The Energy Song
Copyright © 2021 by Erika Goodman

All rights reserved. No part of this publication may be reproduced, distributed, or transmitted in any form or by any means, including photocopying, recording, or other electronic or mechanical methods, without the prior written permission of the author, except in the case of brief quotations embodied in critical reviews and certain other non-commercial uses permitted by copyright law.

tellwell

Tellwell Talent
www.tellwell.ca

ISBN
978-0-2288-6004-4 (Hardcover)
978-0-2288-4879-0 (Paperback)
978-0-2288-5083-0 (eBook)

For information about special discounts for bulk purchases, or to book Erika for a live event, please contact the author directly at erikagimli@hotmail.com.

# THE ENERGY SONG

By Erika Goodman

Illustrated by Maja Larson and Samantha Don

Before you begin:

The Energy referred to in this book is also known as biofield, bioenergetic field, universal energy, chi, prana, consciousness, or the Force. This subtle energy constantly flows through your body and connects you to the universe. In it contains all possibilities.

The Energy Song is an introduction to experiencing this energy.

French version translation provided by Translation Agency of Manitoba.

Music score application used for sheet music: Crescendo Music Notation Editor.

Disclaimer: The Energy Song should only be done in a safe, risk-free, comfortable environment. Neither the author nor the publisher shall be liable for any loss or damage to property, health or life allegedly arising from any suggestion in this book.

Dear Curious Ones,

This is not just a book, this is not just a song,
This will change what you thought of the world all along.

With a slap and a grin and a twist, twist, twist,
You'll open yourself to the energy you've missed!

If the world is too big and you feel too small
Use <u>The Energy Song</u> to balance it all!

Learn the song, feel it and share it with everyone!
Energy is endless! It's healing, helpful, free and fun!

Be Well!
Erika Goodman

Slap your hands together,

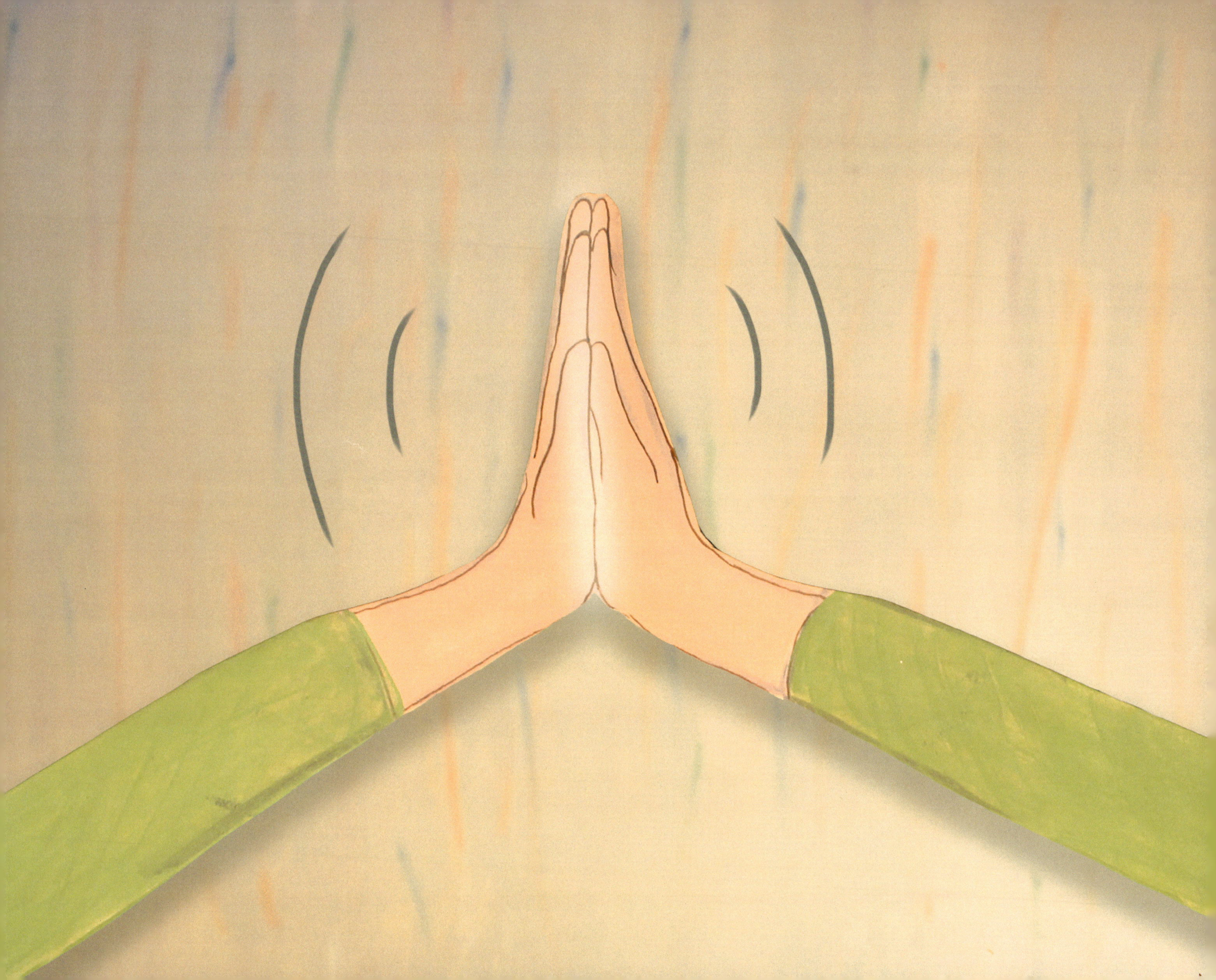

Rub them up and down.

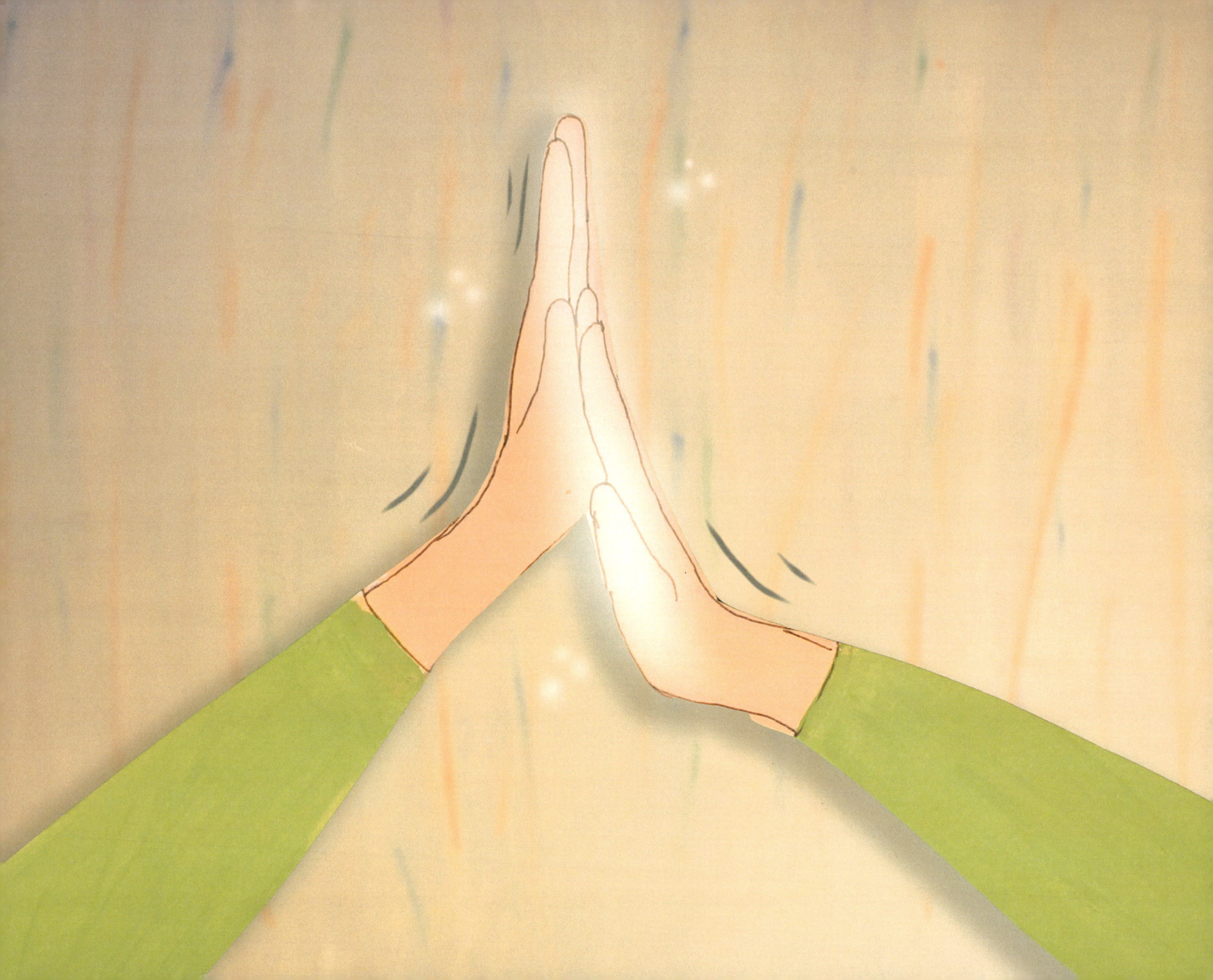

Take a happy thought

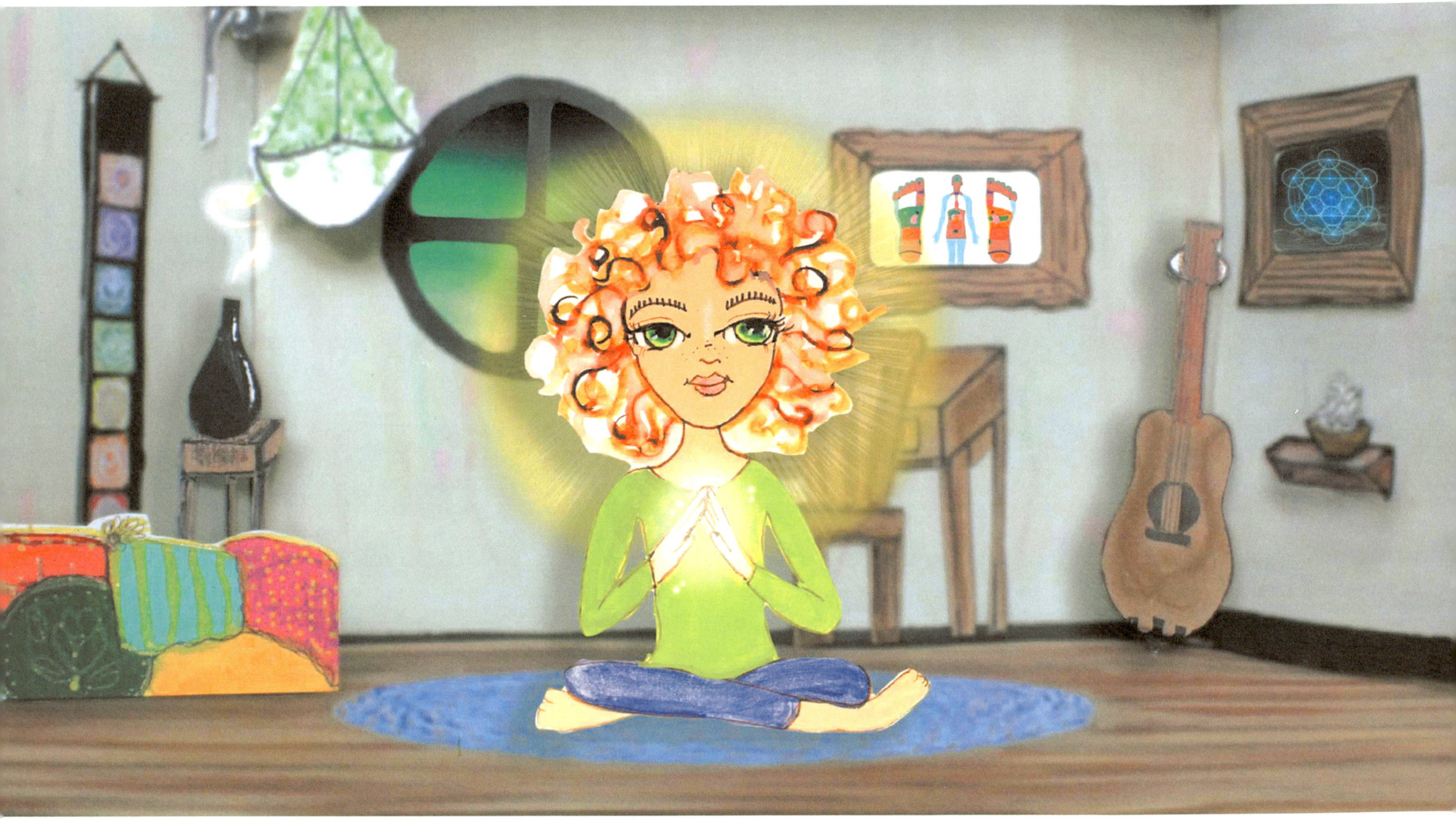

And feel it all around.

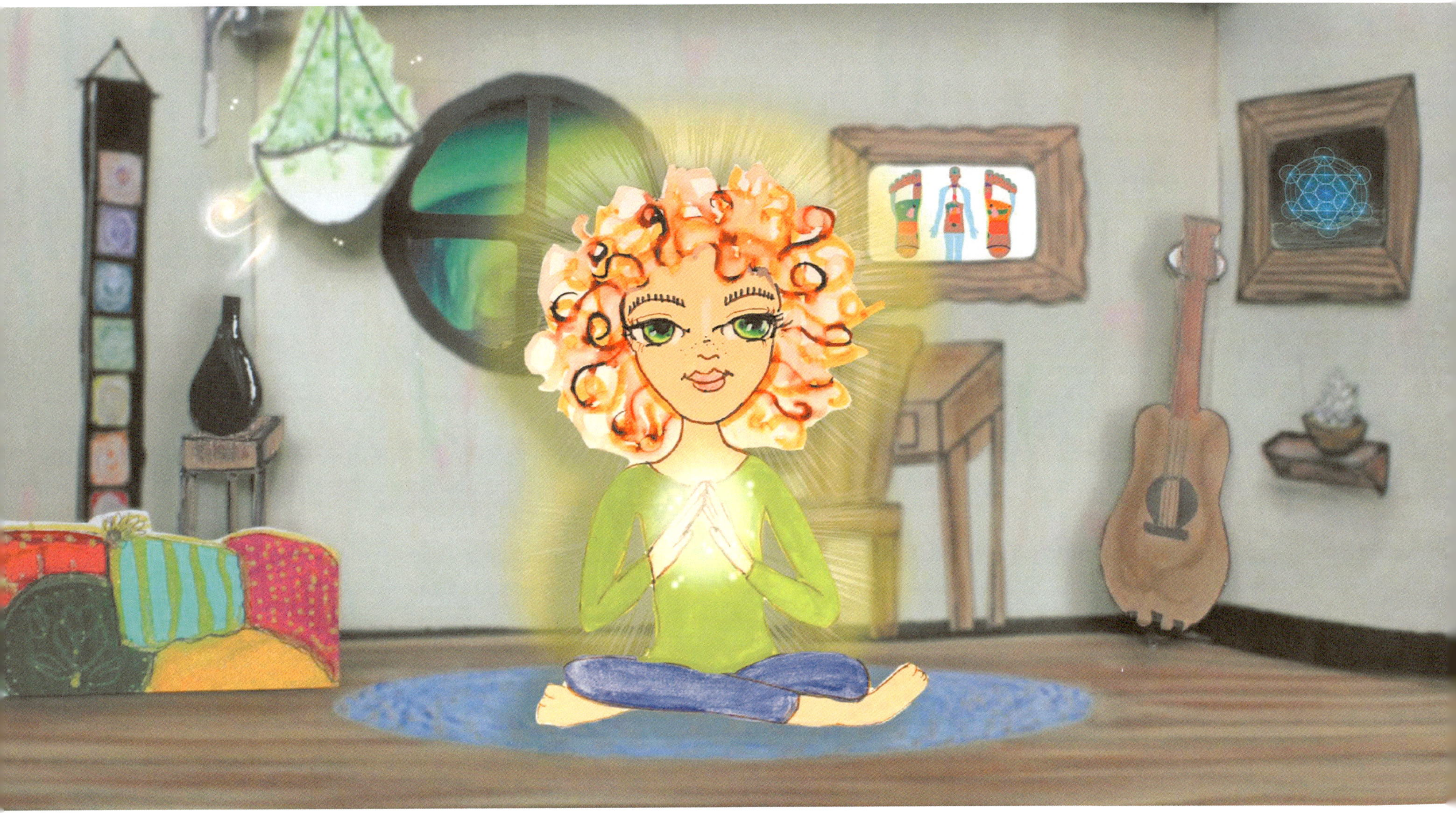

Turn the key, turn the key.

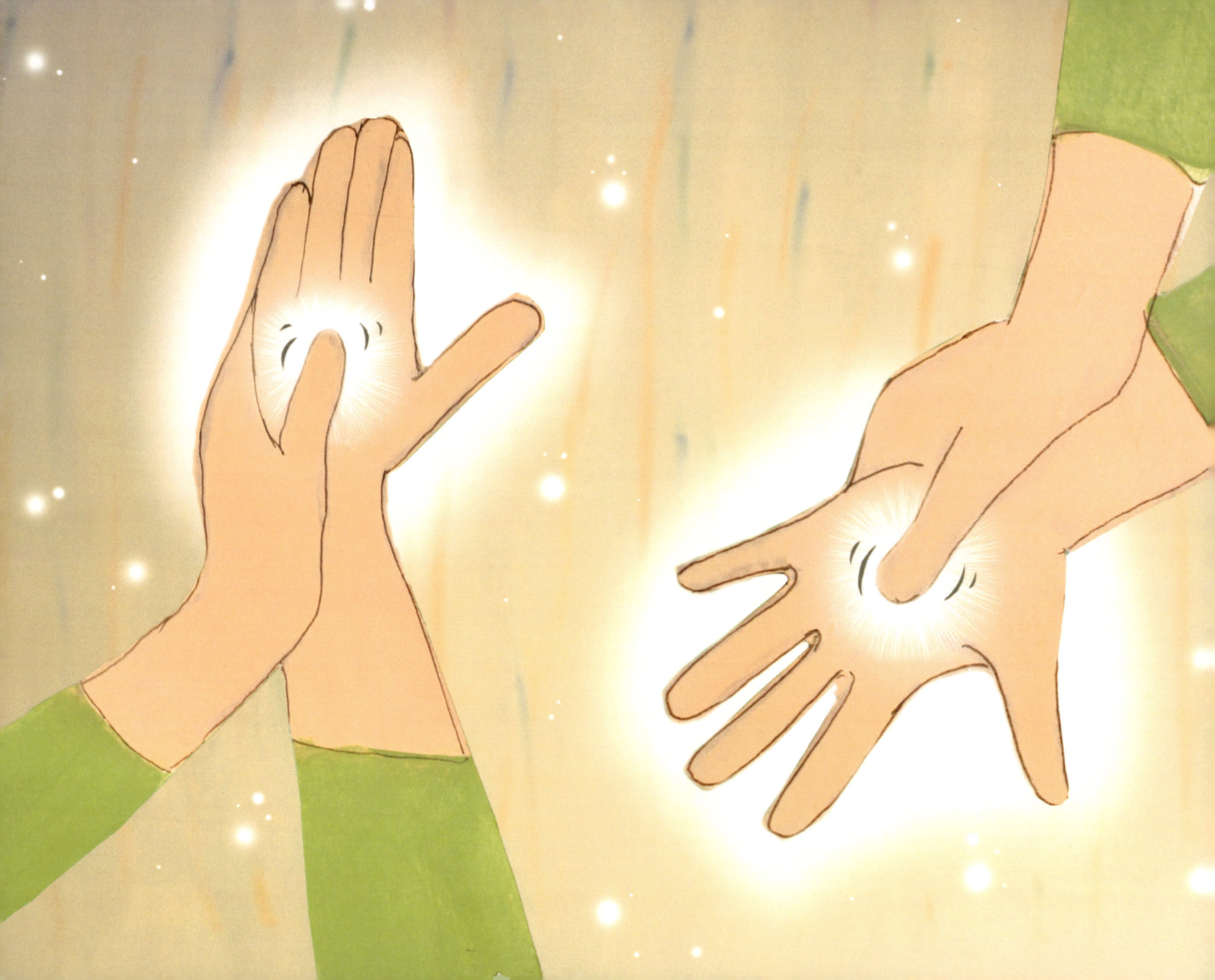

Take a deep breath and face your hands apart,

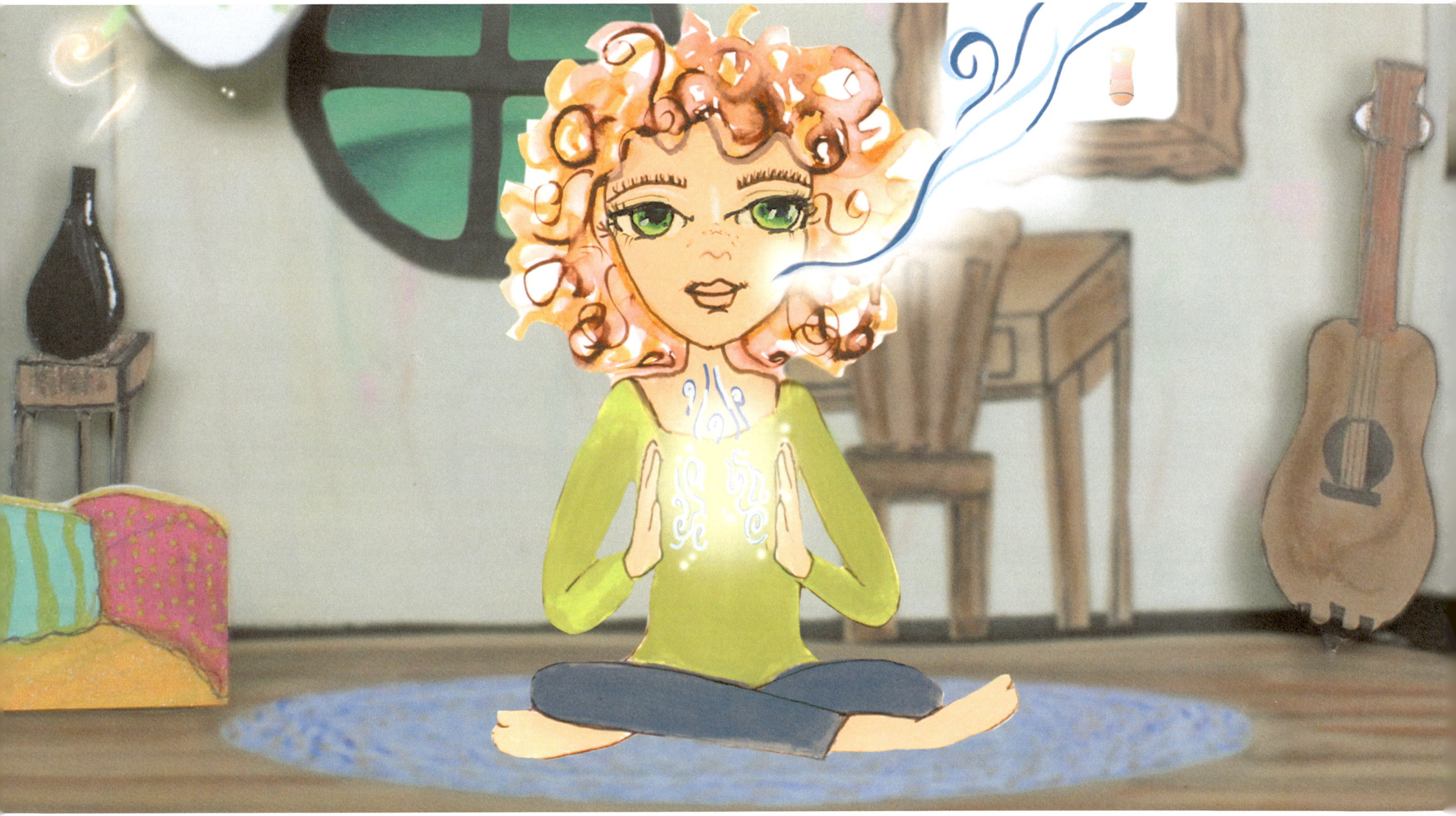

Close your eyes and open your heart.

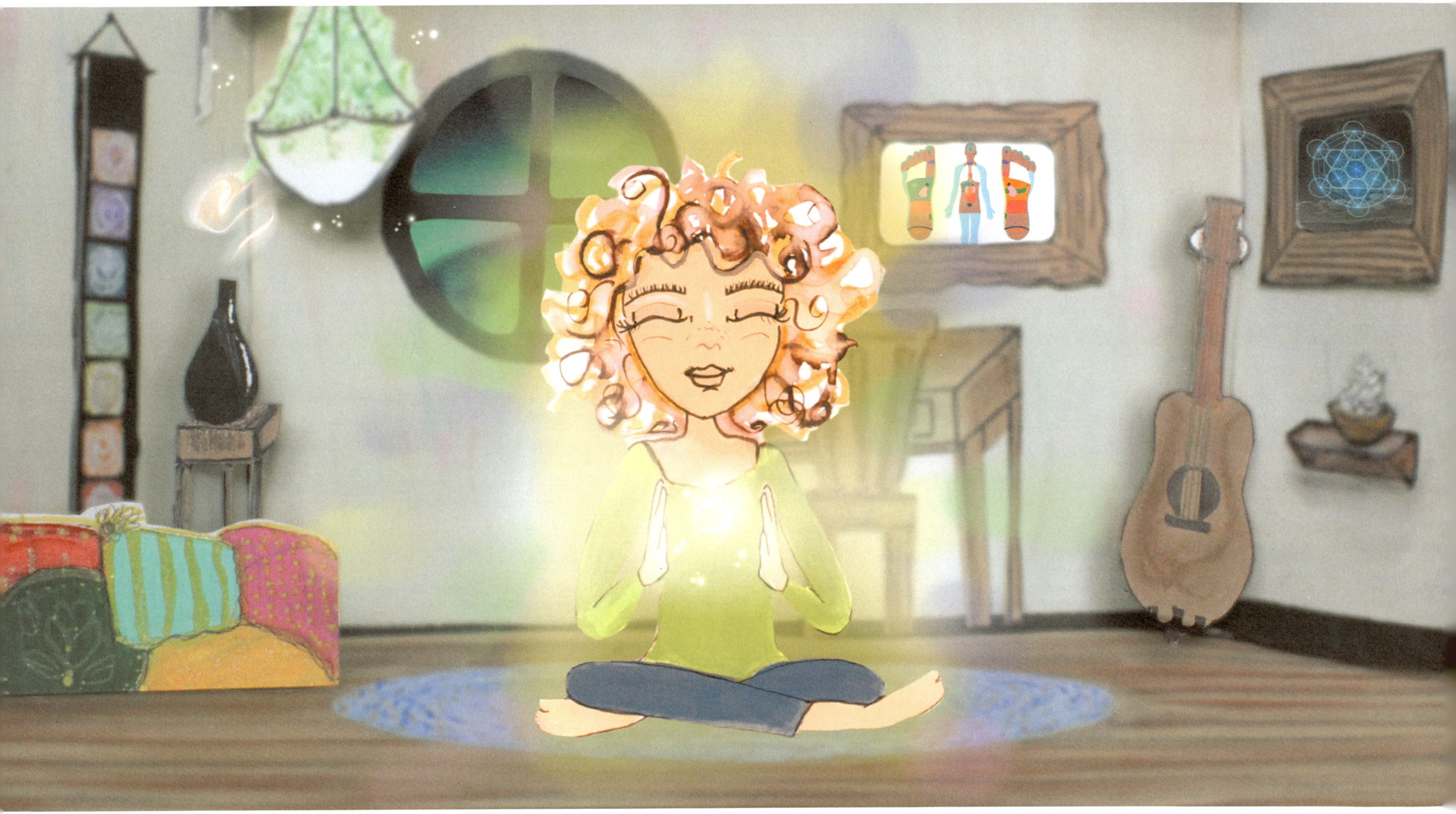

Slowly squeezing in,

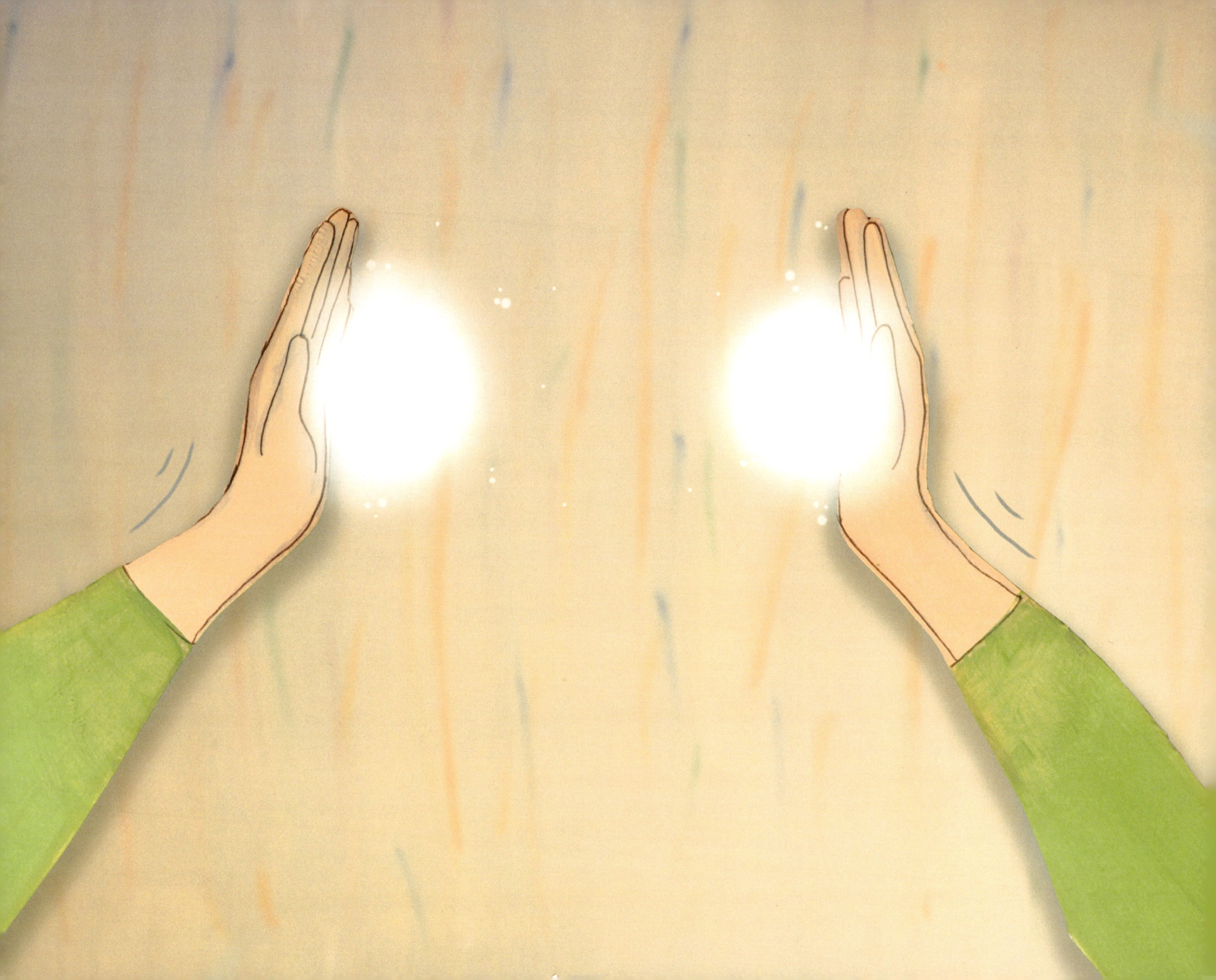

Slowly squeezing in,

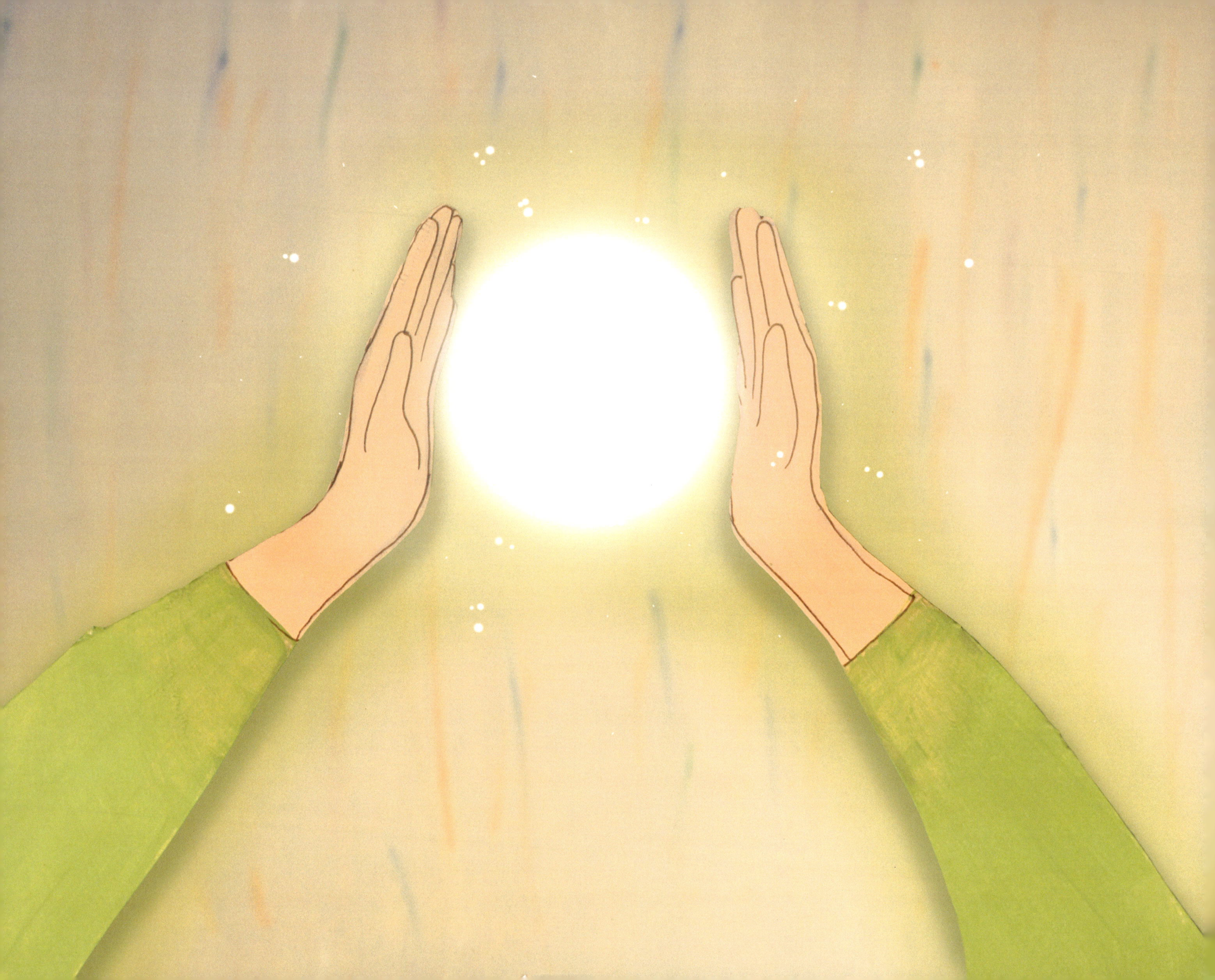

I can feel my energy flowing out and in.

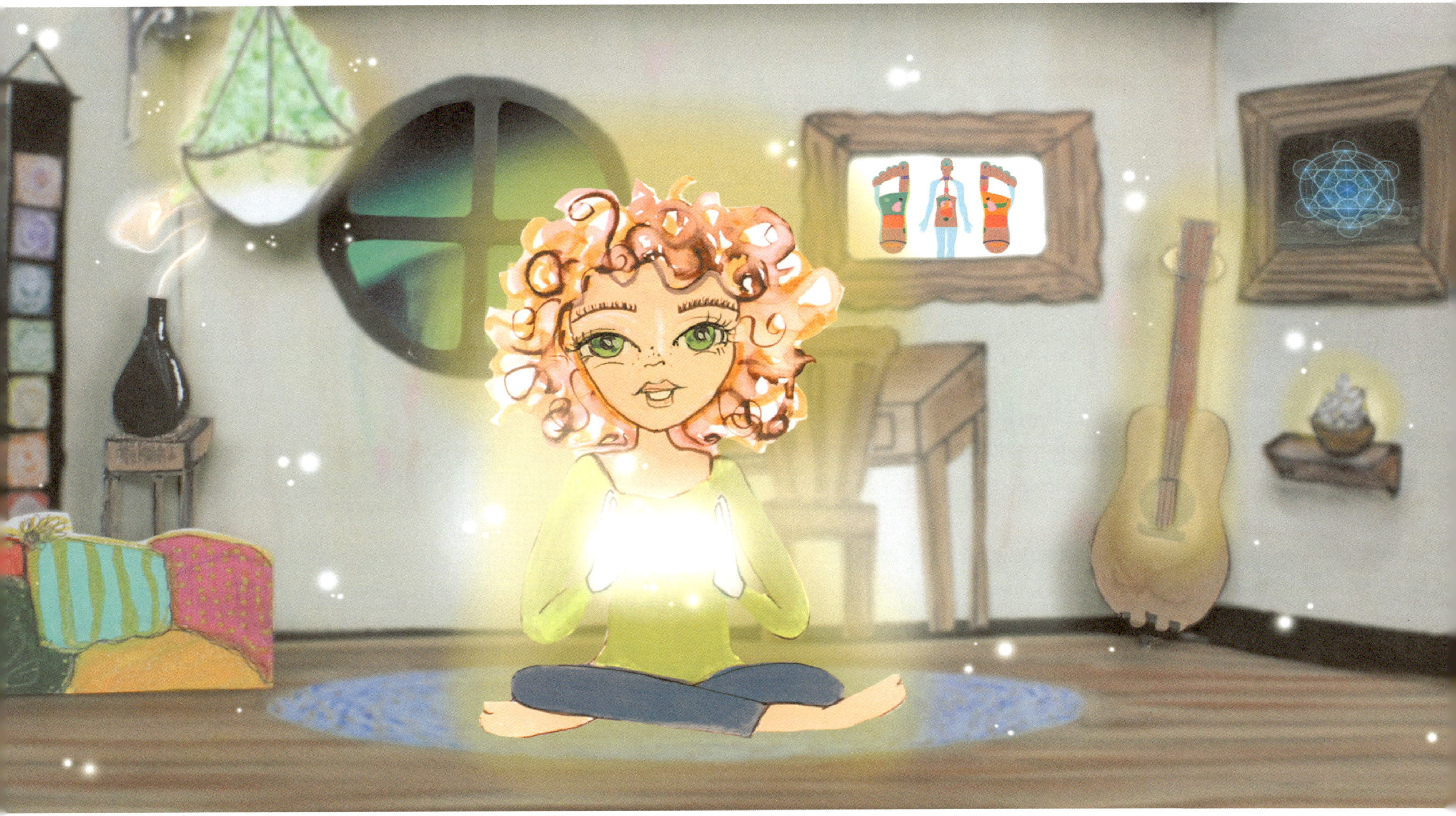

I can feel my energy flowing out and in.

# The Energy Song
## *La chanson de l'énergie*

Composed by Erika Goodman

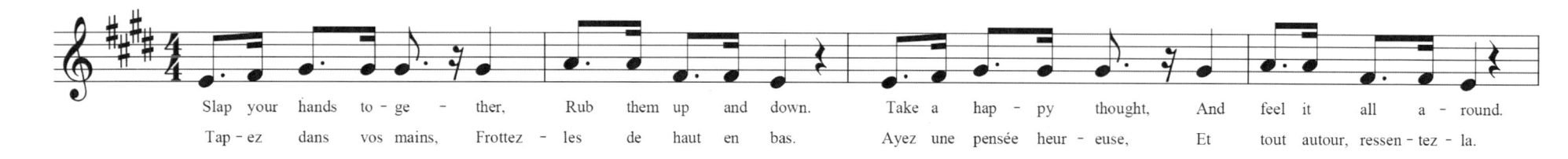

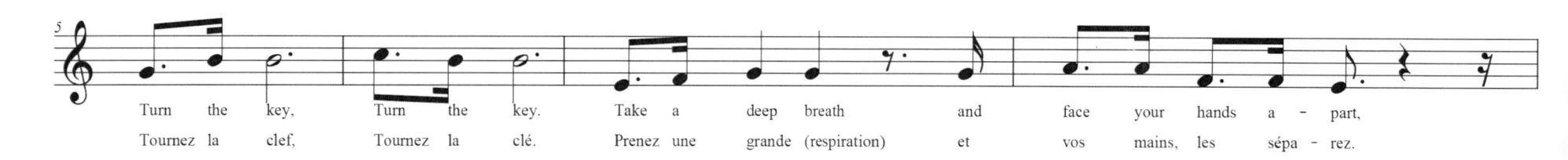

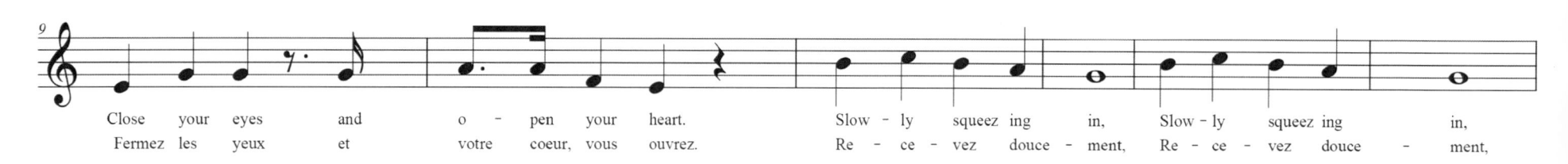

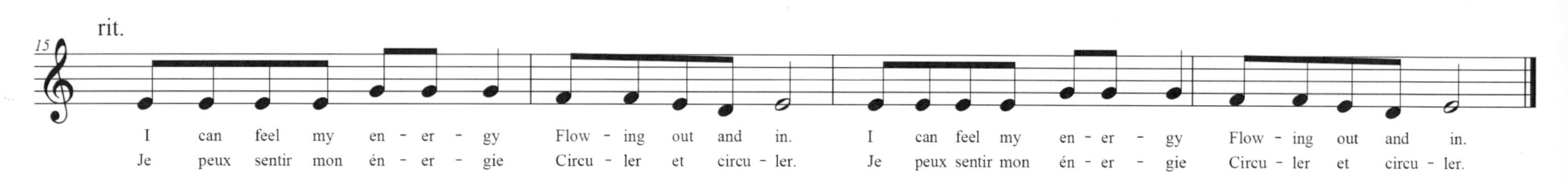

Slap your hands to - ge - ther, Rub them up and down. Take a hap - py thought, And feel it all a - round.
Tap - ez dans vos mains, Frottez - les de haut en bas. Ayez une pensée heur - euse, Et tout autour, ressen - tez - la.

Turn the key, Turn the key. Take a deep breath and face your hands a - part,
Tournez la clef, Tournez la clé. Prenez une grande (respiration) et vos mains, les sépa - rez.

Close your eyes and o - pen your heart. Slow - ly squeez ing in, Slow - ly squeez ing in,
Fermez les yeux et votre coeur, vous ouvrez. Re - ce - vez douce - ment, Re - ce - vez douce - ment,

*rit.*

I can feel my en - er - gy Flow - ing out and in. I can feel my en - er - gy Flow - ing out and in.
Je peux sentir mon én - er - gie Circu - ler et circu - ler. Je peux sentir mon én - er - gie Circu - ler et circu - ler.

*Helpful Hints*

Keep your elbows out.

Go slowly.

Breathe.

Relax, especially your hands.

Happier thoughts!

Don't force it, just allow it.

Practice the song until you memorize it, then use it anytime!

What does your energy feel like?

What will you do with it?

For more information, activities, and ideas, see the author's website at erikagoodman.ca.

CPSIA information can be obtained
at www.ICGtesting.com
Printed in the USA
LVRC101646161021
700650LV00003B/50